Piano Solo

CHRISTMAS JAZZ FOR SOLO PIANO

8 Spicy Settings by Craig Curry

ISBN 978-1-4803-8774-4

HAL•LEONARD® CORPORATION
7777 W. BLUEMOUND RD. P.O.BOX 13819 MILWAUKEE, WI 53213

In Australia Contact:
Hal Leonard Australia Pty. Ltd.
4 Lentara Court
Cheltenham, Victoria, 3192 Australia
Email: ausadmin@halleonard.com.au

Visit Hal Leonard Online at
www.halleonard.com

COME, THOU LONG-EXPECTED JESUS

Words by CHARLES WESLEY
Music by ROWLAND HUGH PRICHARD
Arranged by Craig Curry

Happy, relaxed Jazz Waltz ♩ = 132

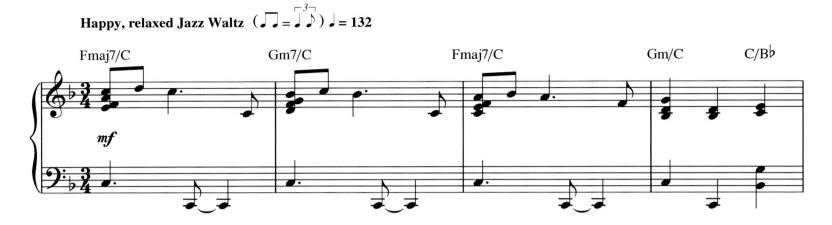

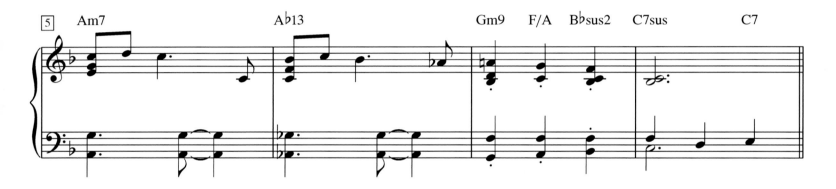

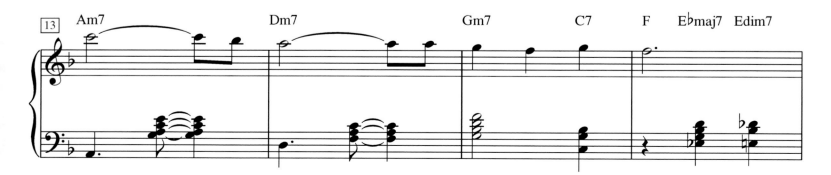

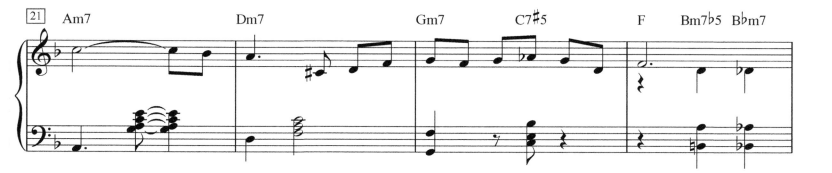

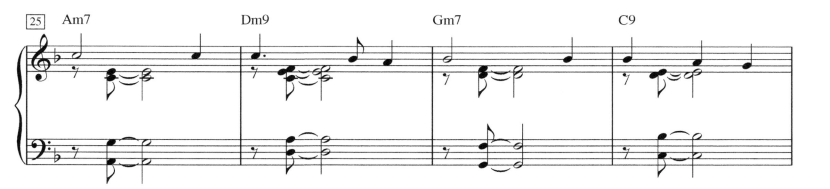

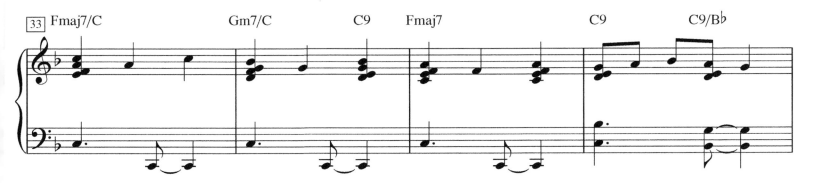

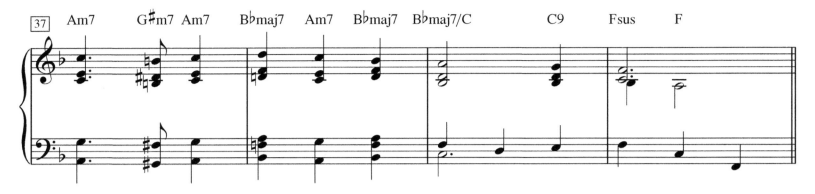

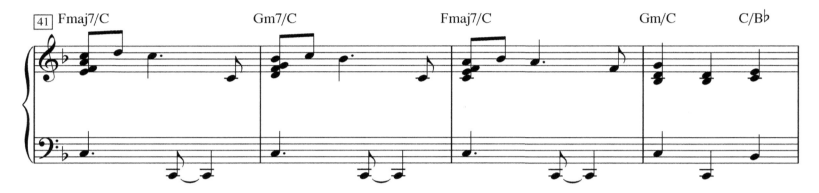

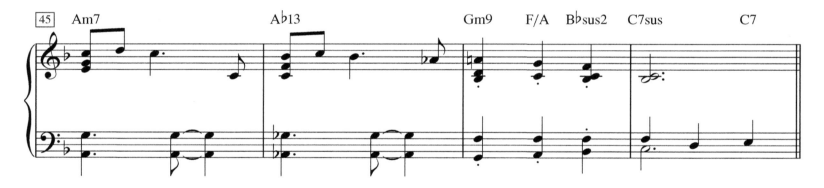

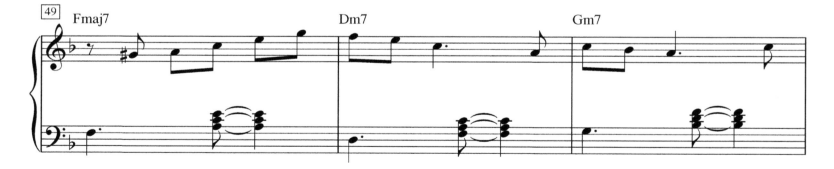

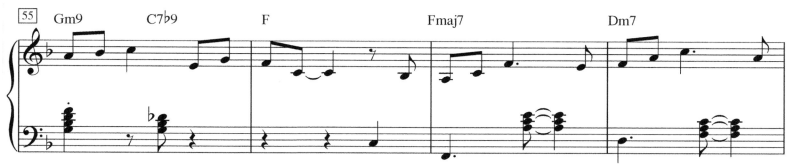

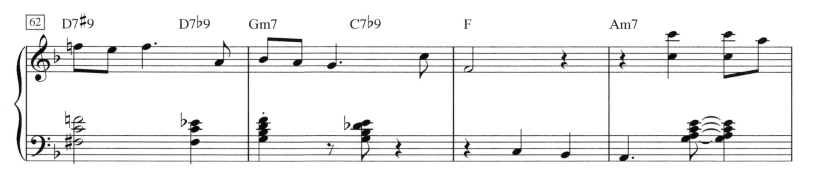

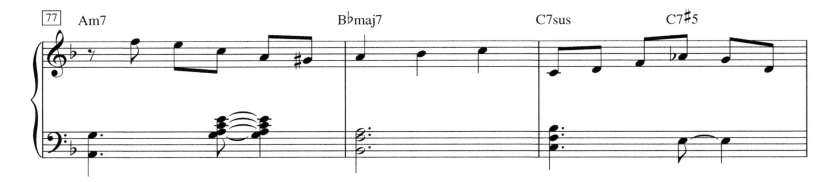

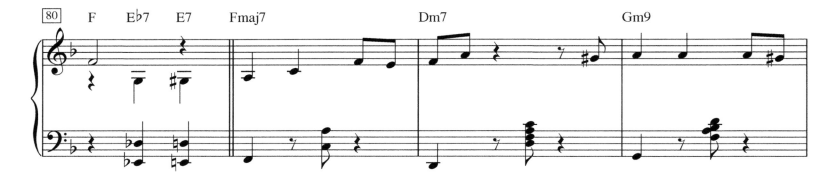

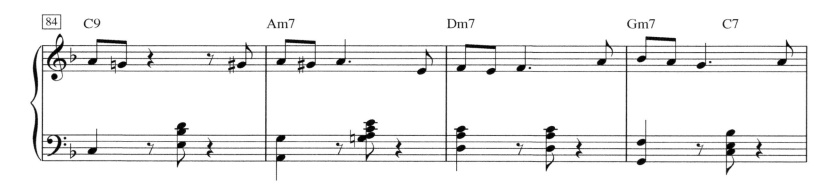

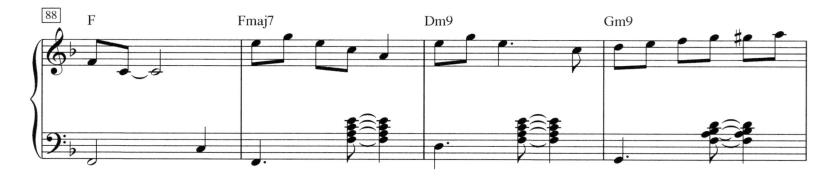

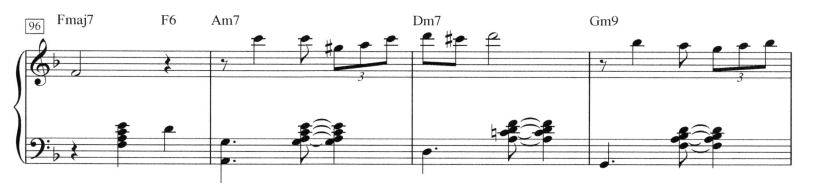

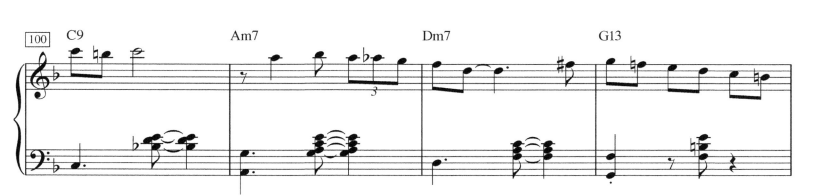

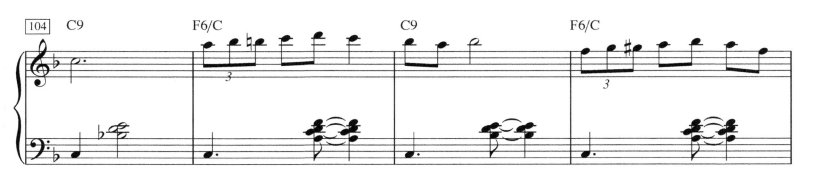

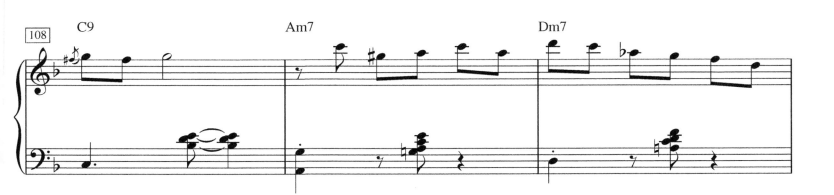

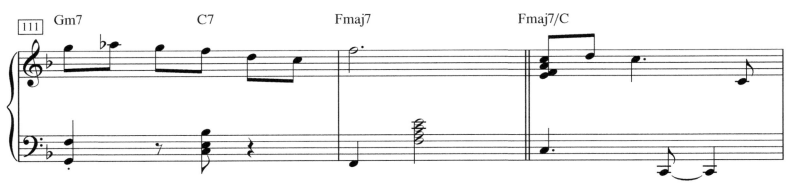

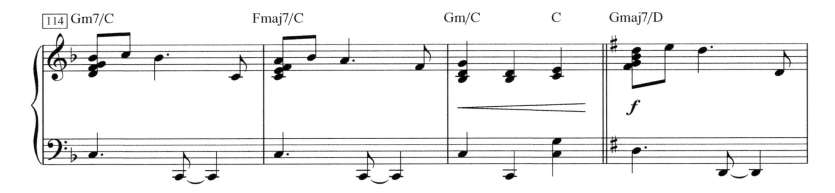

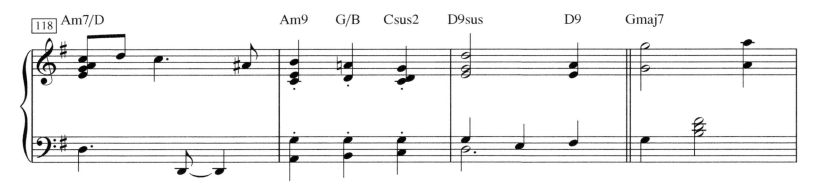

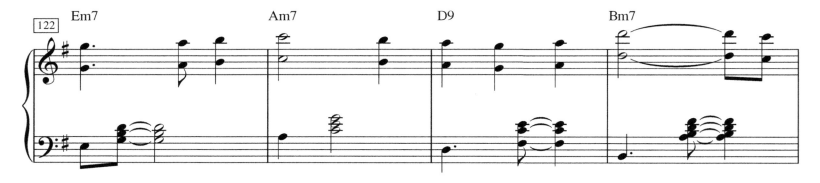

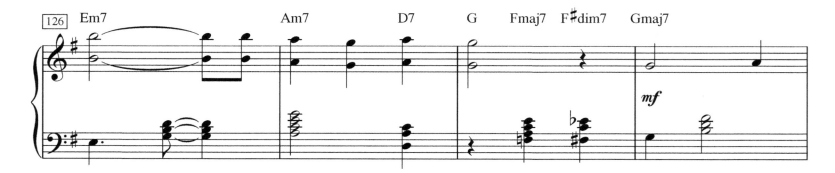

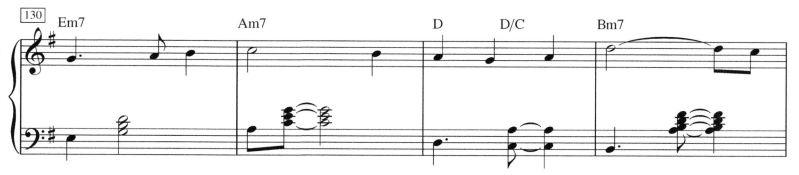

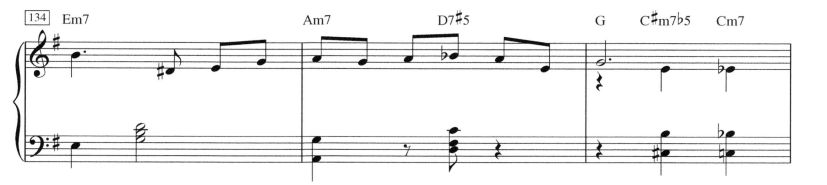

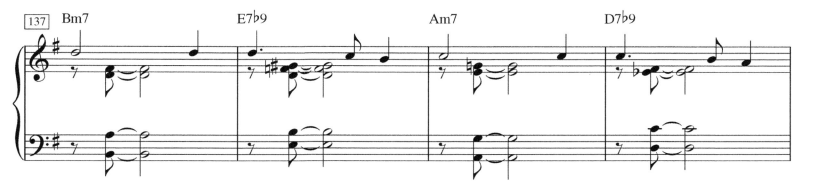

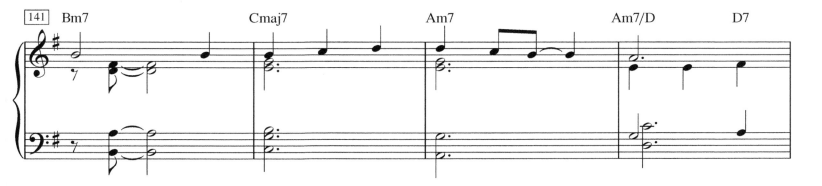

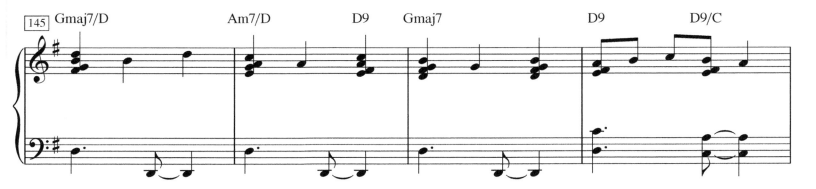

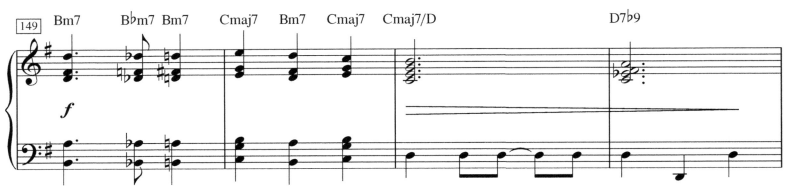

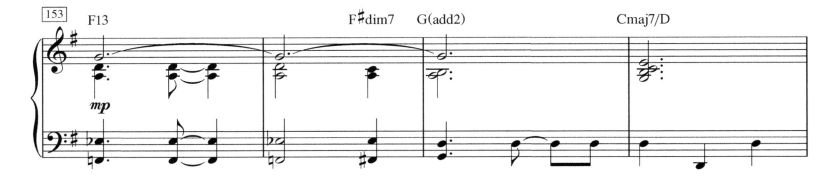

I HEARD THE BELLS ON CHRISTMAS DAY

Words by HENRY WADSWORTH LONGFELLOW
Music by JOHN BAPTISTE CALKIN
Arranged by Craig Curry

Slowly, rubato ♩ = ca. 60

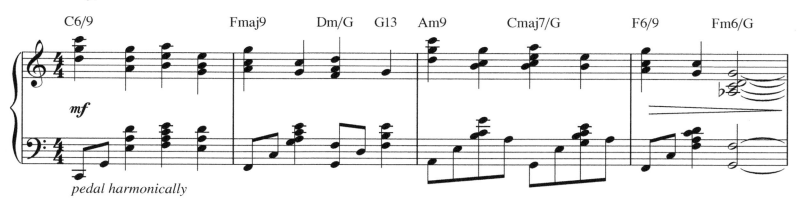

pedal harmonically

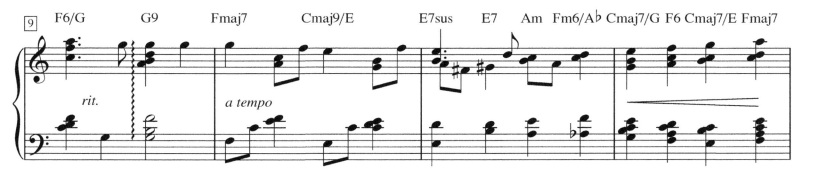

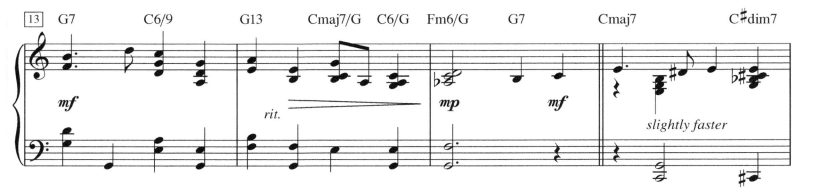

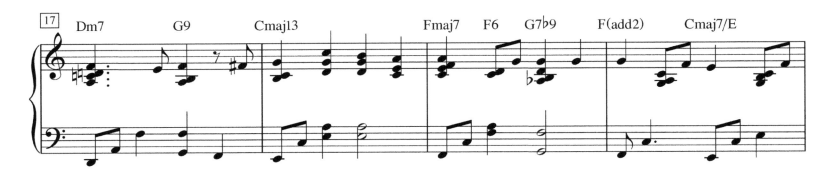

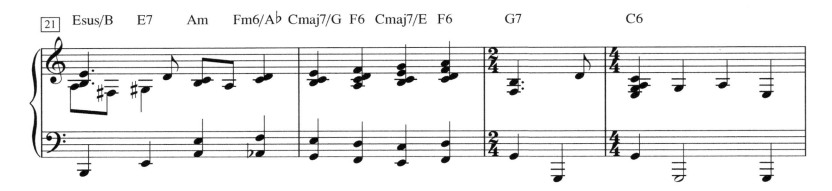

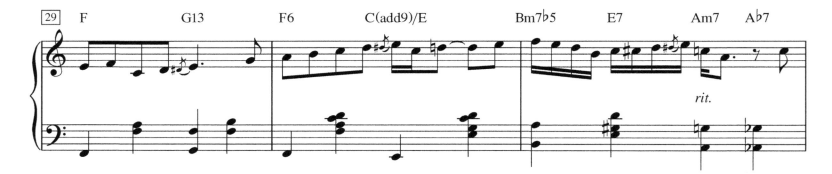

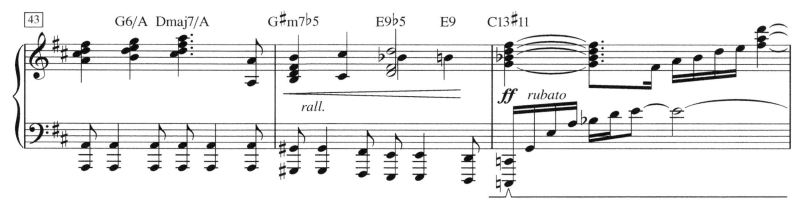

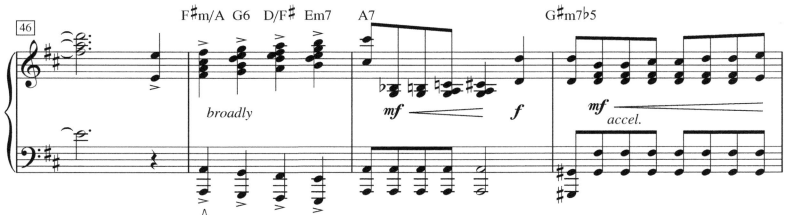

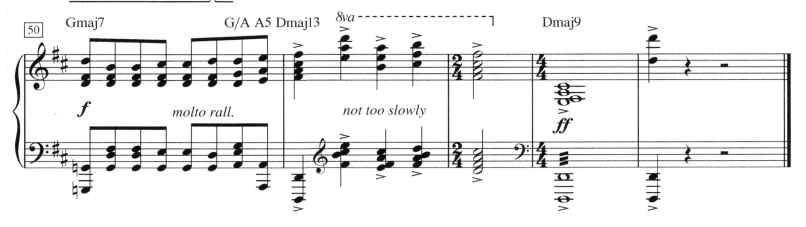

DANCE OF THE SUGAR PLUM FAIRY
from THE NUTCRACKER

By PYOTR IL'YICH TCHAIKOVSKY
Arranged by Craig Curry

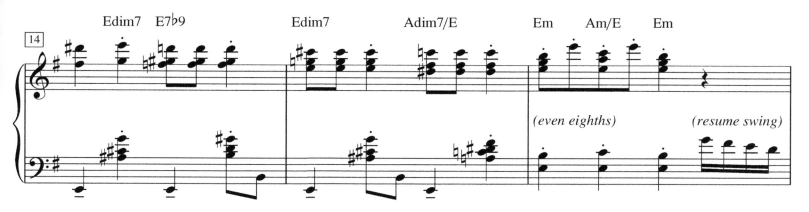

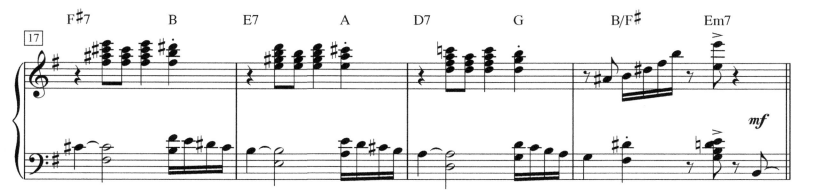

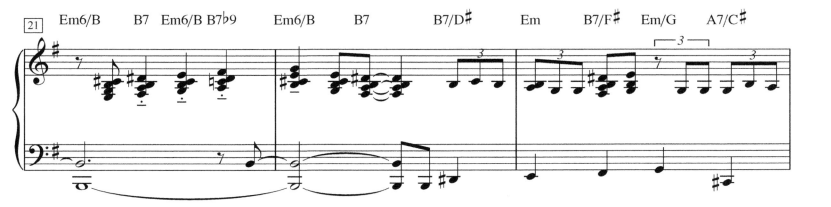

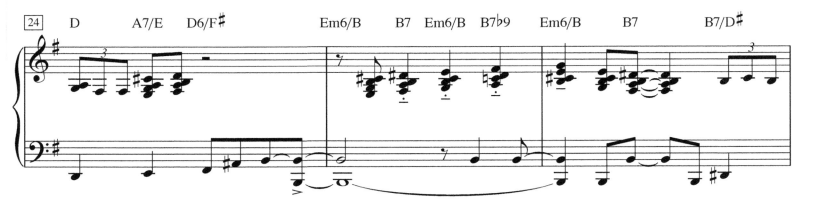

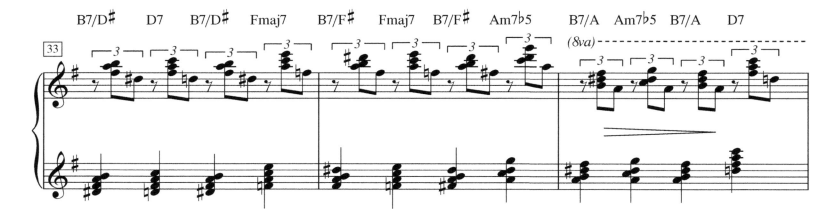

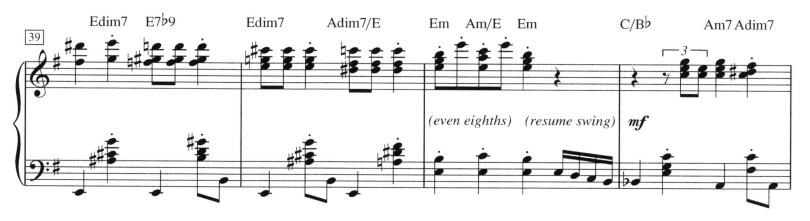

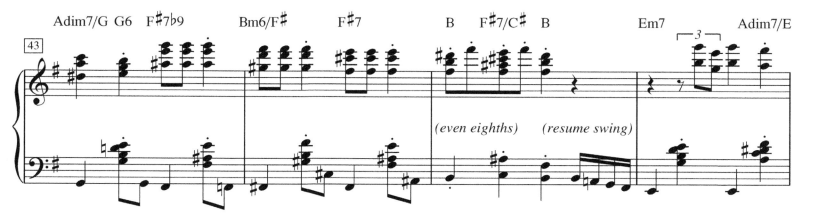

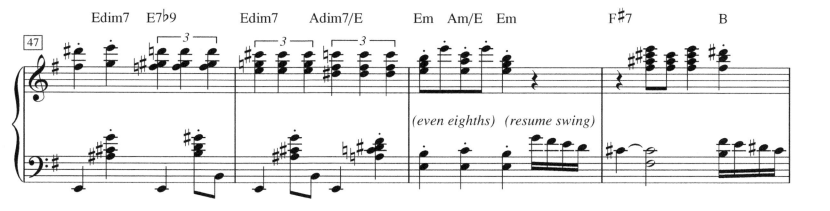

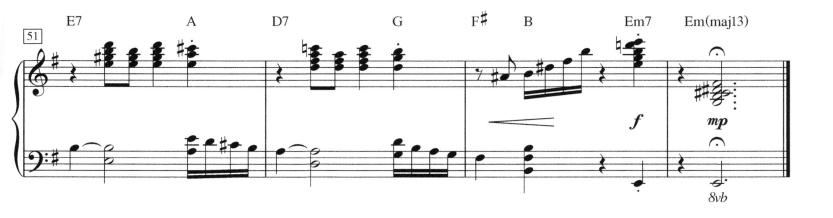

GOD REST YE MERRY, GENTLEMEN

19th Century English Carol
Arranged by Craig Curry

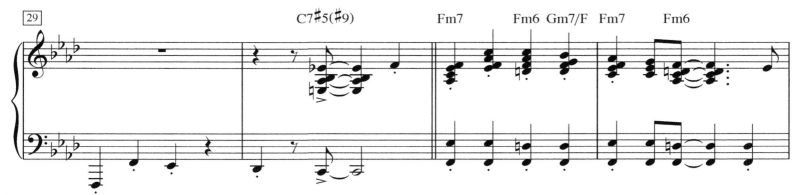

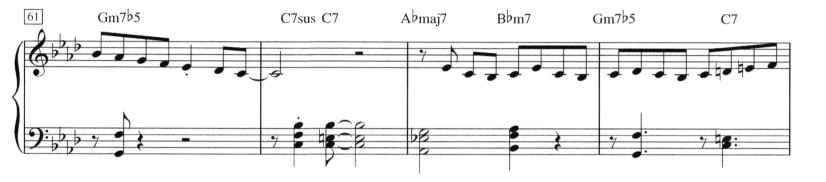

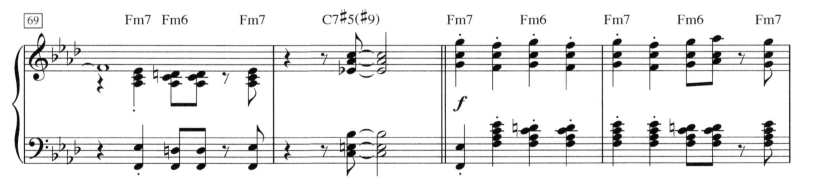

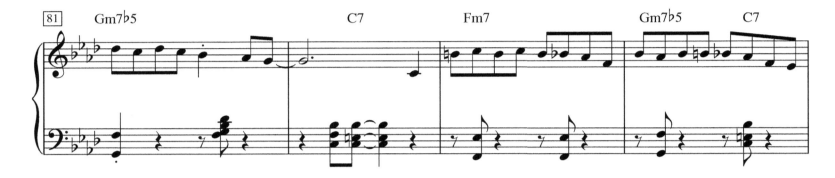

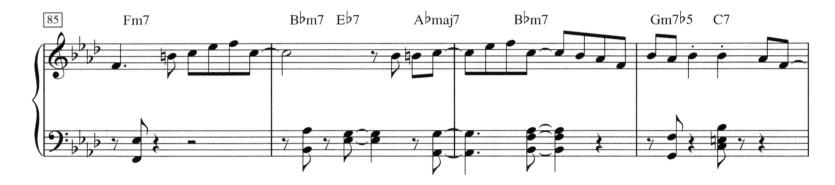

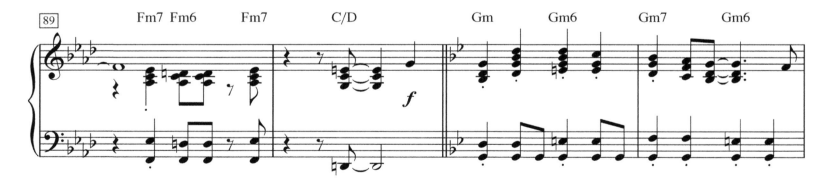

IN THE BLEAK MIDWINTER

Poem by CHRISTINA ROSSETTI
Music by GUSTAV HOLST
Arranged by Craig Curry

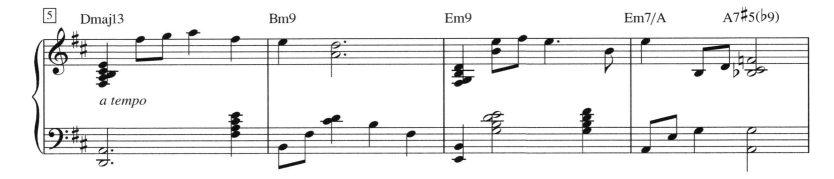

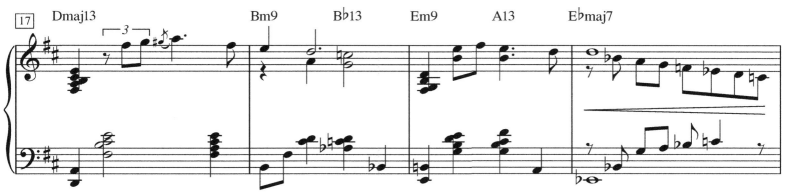

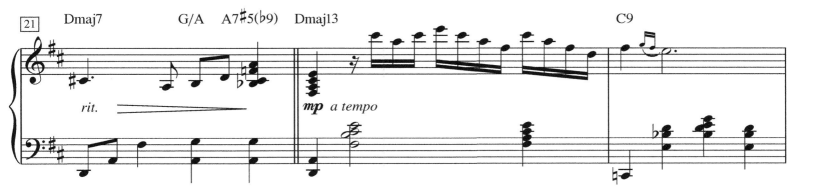

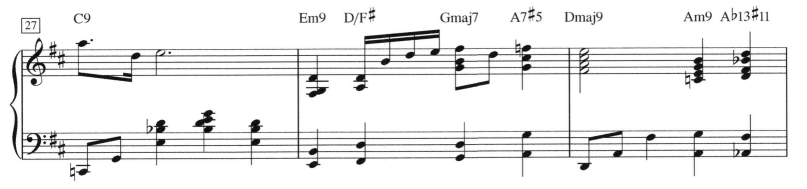

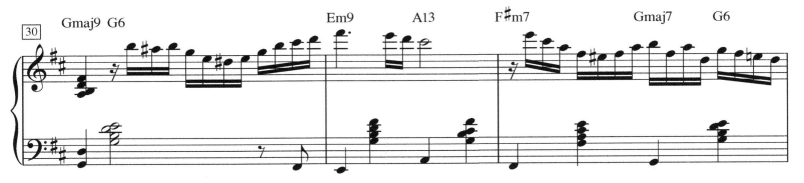

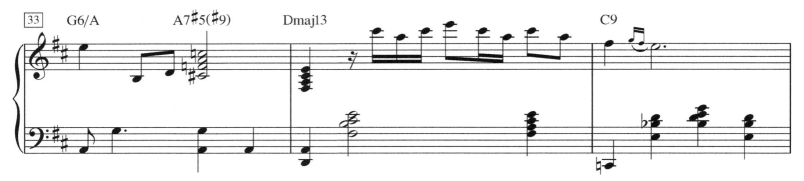

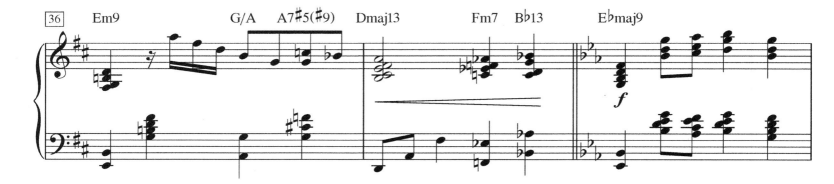

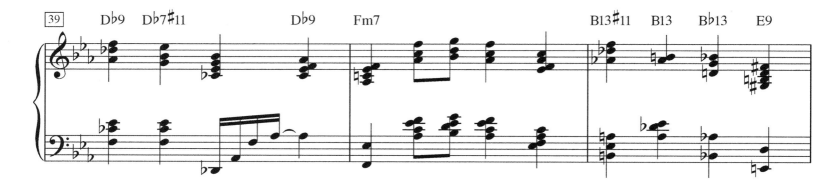

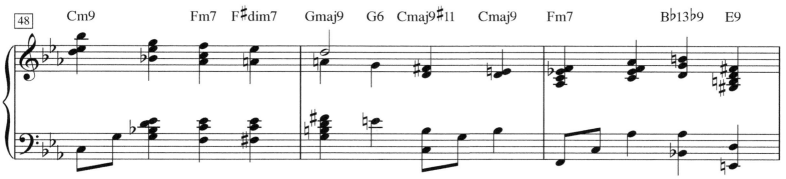

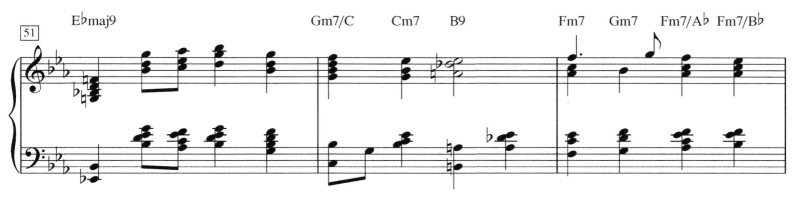

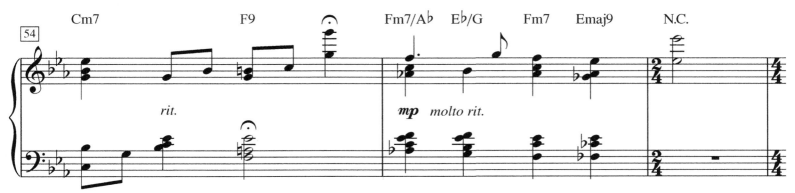

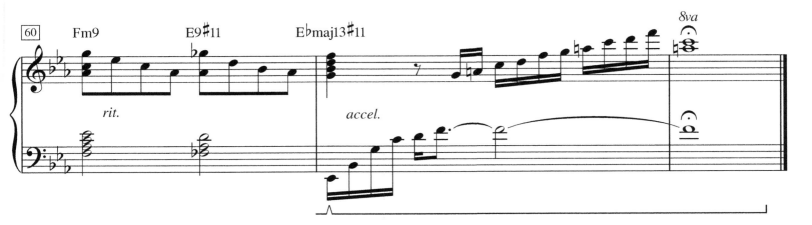

SILENT NIGHT

for Jennifer Whitfield

Words by JOSEPH MOHR
Music by FRANZ X. GRUBER
Arranged by Craig Curry

Funk-Rock groove, with attitude ♩ = 136

L.H. plays 8vb throughout

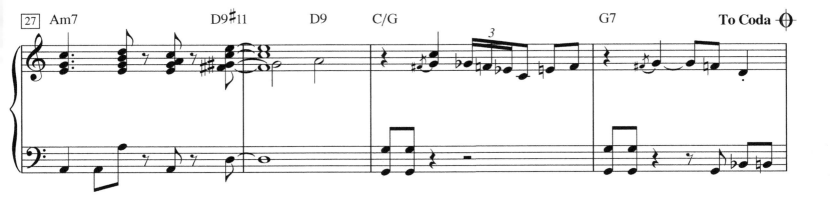

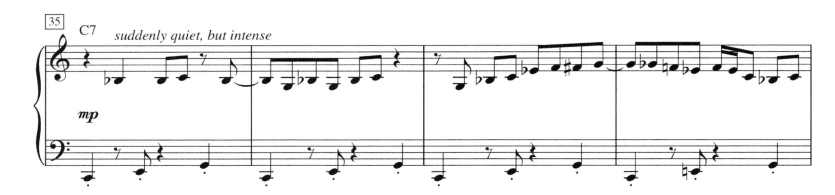

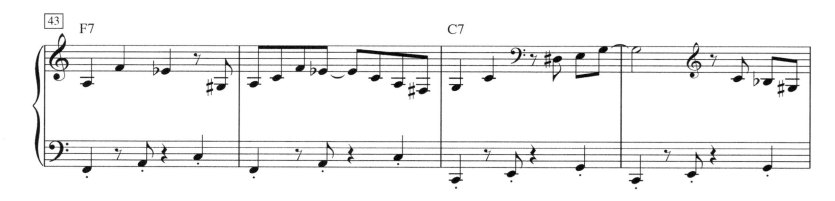

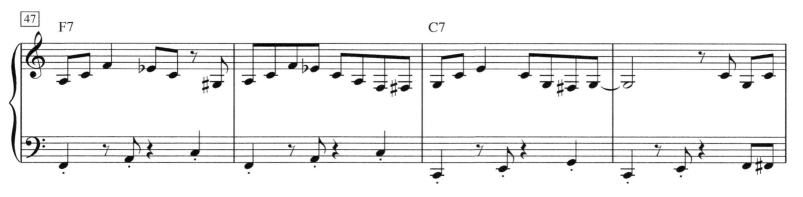

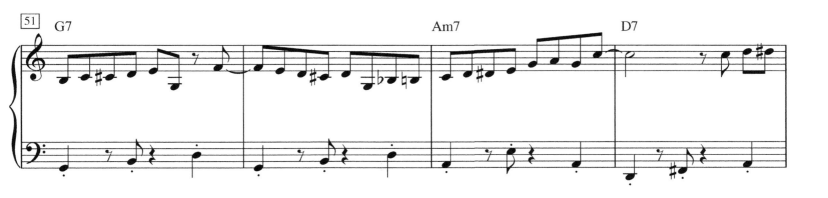

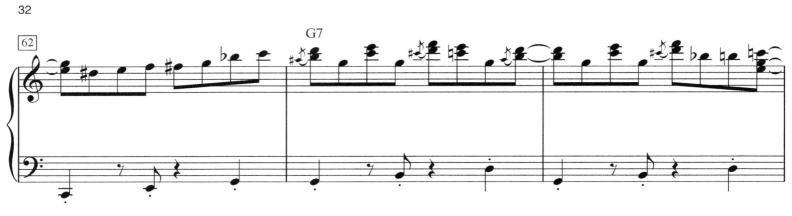

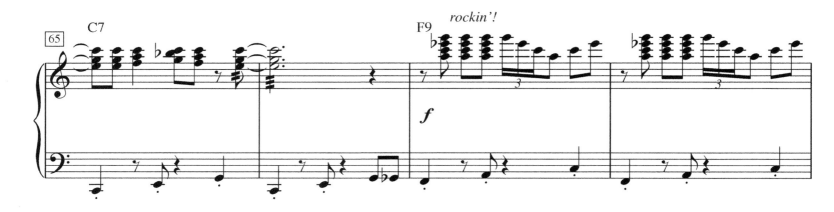

D.S. al Coda

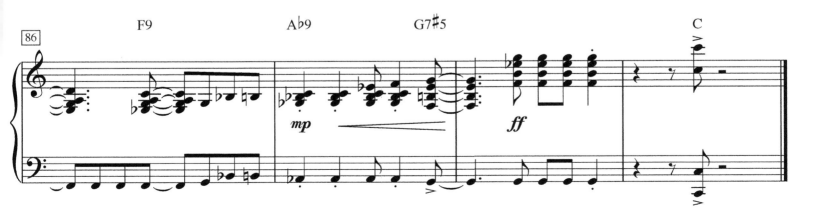

WE THREE KINGS OF ORIENT ARE

Words and Music by JOHN H. HOPKINS, JR.
Arranged by Craig Curry

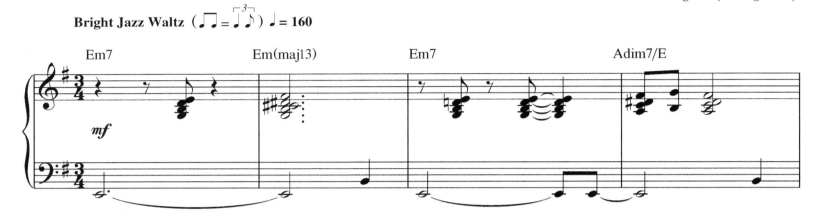

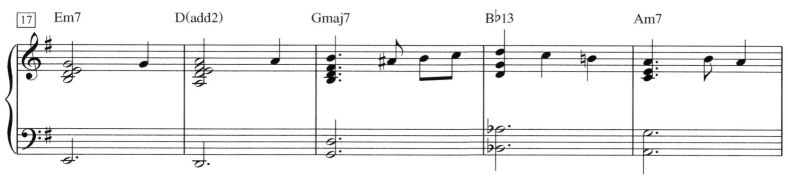

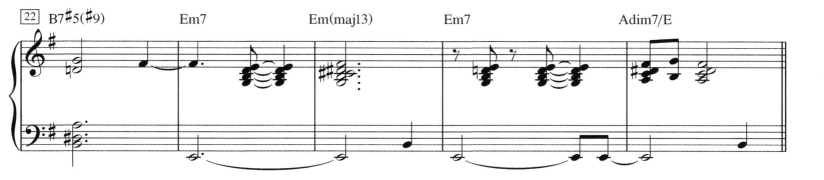

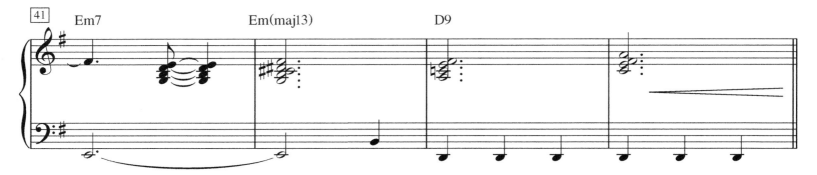

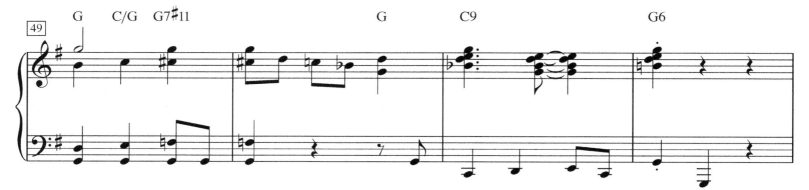

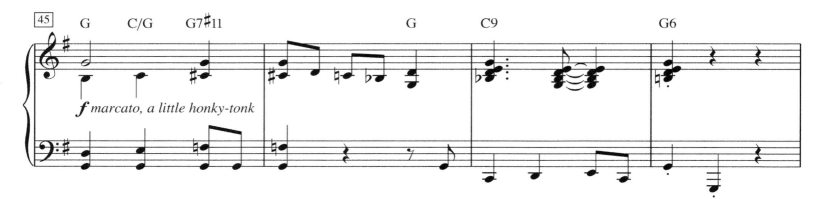

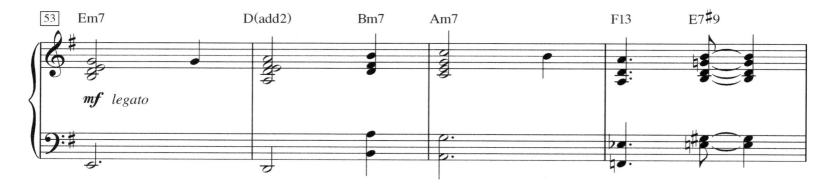

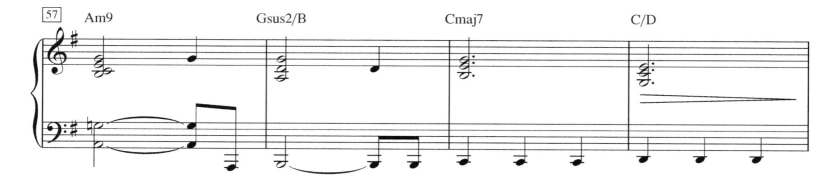

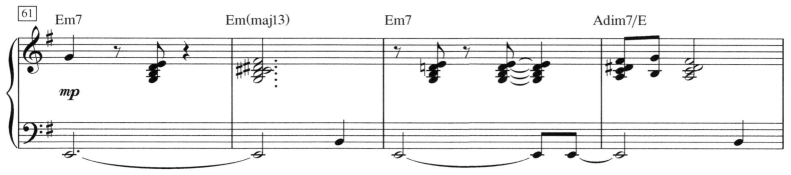

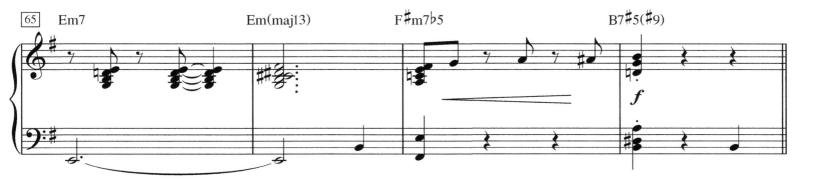

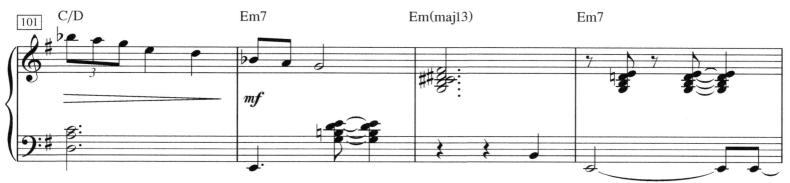

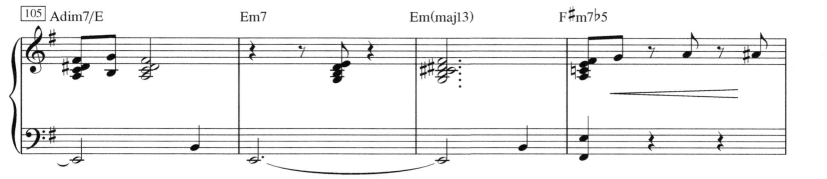

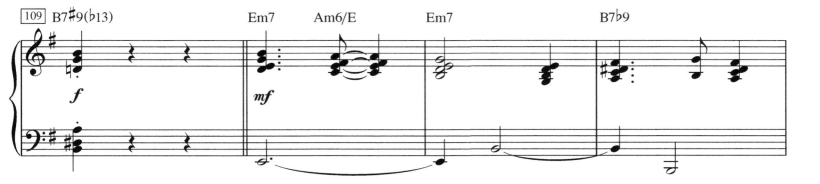

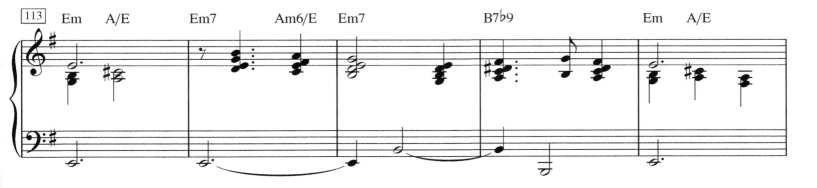

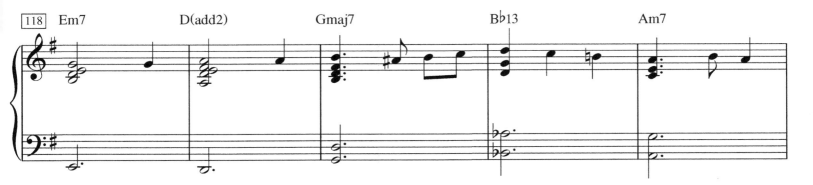

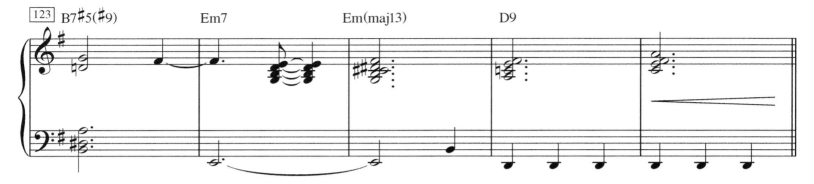

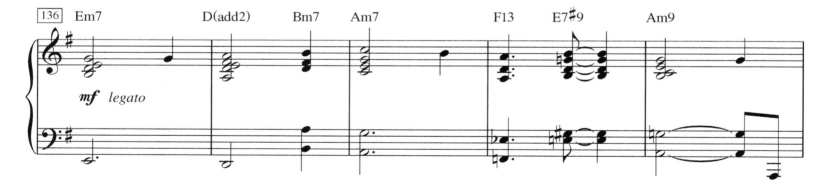

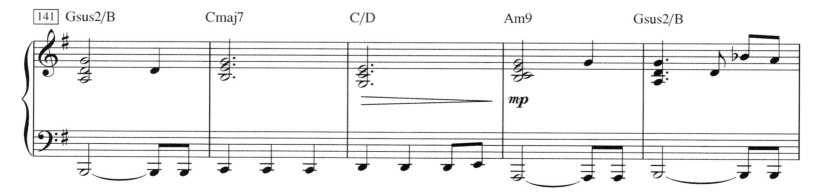

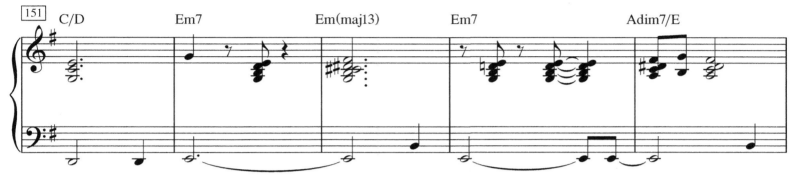

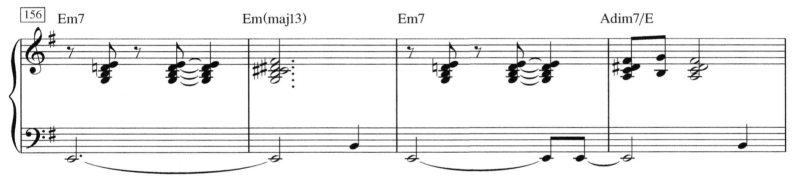

SANTA CLAUS MEDLEY
(Jolly Old St. Nicholas/Up on the Housetop)

Arranged by Craig Curry

Funky, with straight eighths ♩ = 112

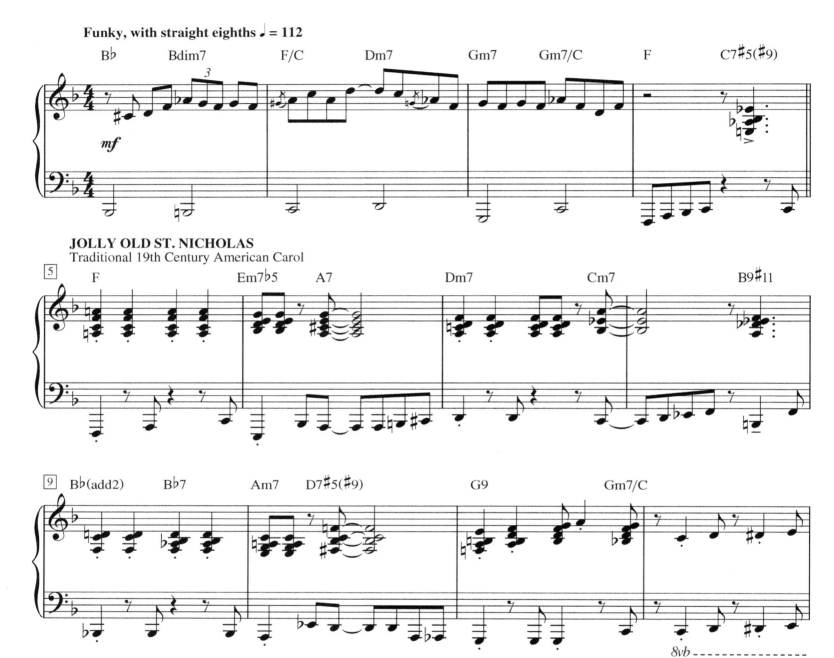

JOLLY OLD ST. NICHOLAS
Traditional 19th Century American Carol

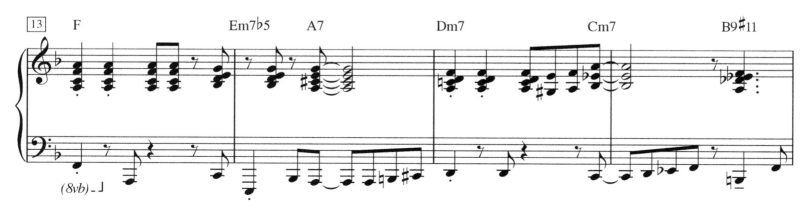

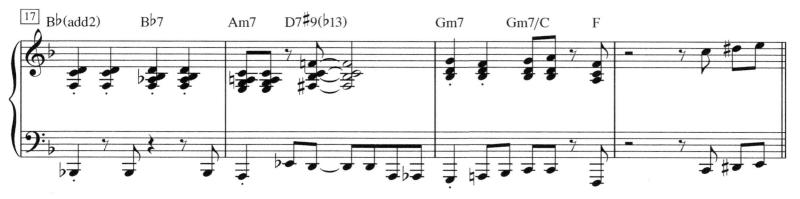

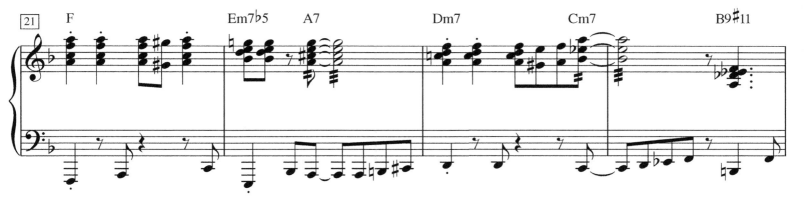

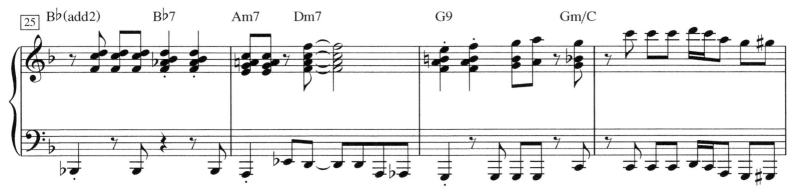

UP ON THE HOUSETOP
Words and Music by B.R. HANBY

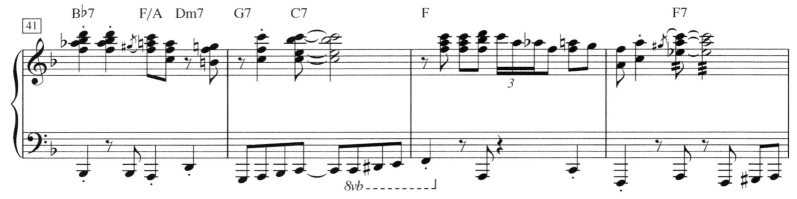

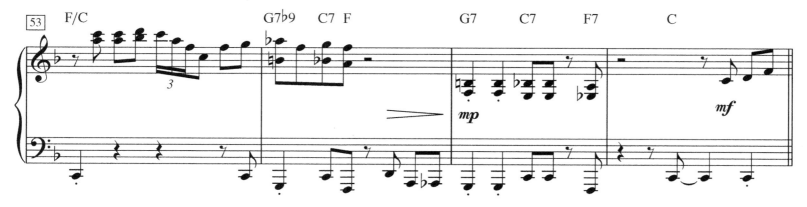

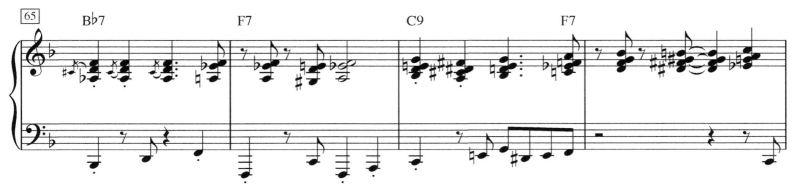

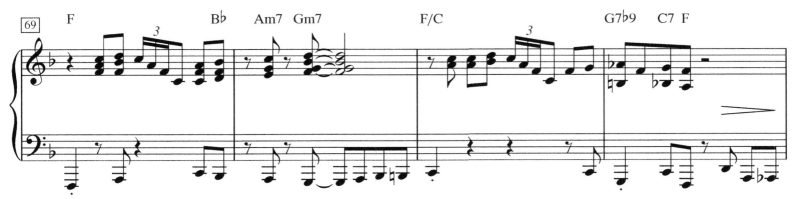

JOLLY OLD ST. NICHOLAS

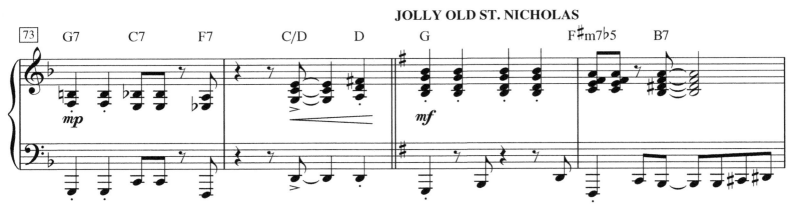

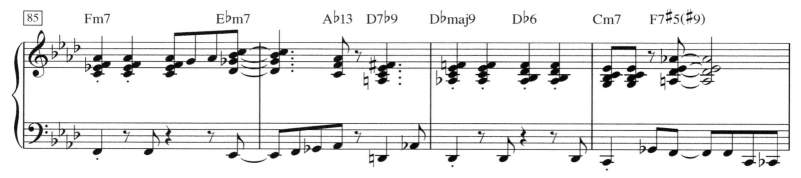

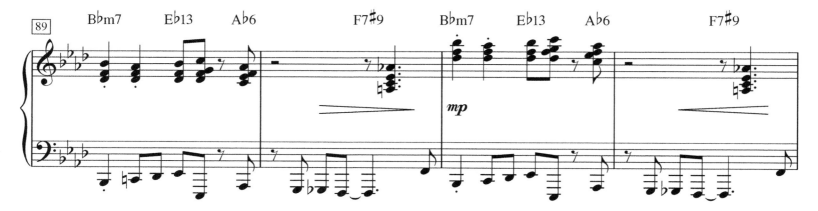

YOUR FAVORITE MUSIC
ARRANGED FOR PIANO SOLO

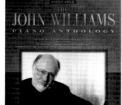

ARTIST, COMPOSER, TV & MOVIE SONGBOOKS

**Adele for Piano Solo –
3rd Edition**
00820186................................$19.99

The Beatles Piano Solo
00294023................................$17.99

**A Charlie Brown
Christmas**
00313176................................$17.99

**Paul Cardall –
The Hymns Collection**
00295925................................$24.99

Coldplay for Piano Solo
00307637................................$17.99

**Selections from
Final Fantasy**
00148699................................$19.99

**Alexis Ffrench – The
Sheet Music Collection**
00345258................................$19.99

Game of Thrones
00199166................................$19.99

Hamilton
00354612................................$19.99

**Hillsong Worship
Favorites**
00303164................................$14.99

How to Train Your Dragon
00138210................................$22.99

Elton John Collection
00306040................................$24.99

La La Land
00283691................................$14.99

John Legend Collection
00233195................................$17.99

Les Misérables
00290271................................$19.99

Little Women
00338470................................$19.99

Outlander: The Series
00254460................................$19.99

**The Peanuts®
Illustrated Songbook**
00313178................................$29.99

**Astor Piazzolla –
Piano Collection**
00285510................................$19.99

**Pirates of the Caribbean –
Curse of the Black Pearl**
00313256................................$19.99

Pride & Prejudice
00123854................................$17.99

Queen
00289784................................$19.99

John Williams Anthology
00194555................................$24.99

George Winston Piano Solos
00306822................................$22.99

MIXED COLLECTIONS

**Beautiful Piano
Instrumentals**
00149926................................$16.99

**Best Jazz
Piano Solos Ever**
00312079................................$24.99

Best Piano Solos Ever
00242928................................$22.99

**Big Book of
Classical Music**
00310508................................$24.99

Big Book of Ragtime Piano
00311749................................$22.99

Christmas Medleys
00350572................................$16.99

Disney Medleys
00242588................................$19.99

Disney Piano Solos
00313128................................$17.99

Favorite Pop Piano Solos
00312523................................$16.99

Great Piano Solos
00311273................................$19.99

**The Greatest Video
Game Music**
00201767................................$19.99

Most Relaxing Songs
00233879................................$17.99

**Movie Themes
Budget Book**
00289137................................$14.99

**100 of the Most Beautiful
Piano Solos Ever**
00102787................................$29.99

100 Movie Songs
00102804................................$29.99

Peaceful Piano Solos
00286009................................$17.99

**Piano Solos for
All Occasions**
00310964................................$24.99

**River Flows in You &
Other Eloquent Songs**
00123854................................$17.99

Sunday Solos for Piano
00311272................................$17.99

Top Hits for Piano Solo
00294635................................$14.99

HAL•LEONARD®
View songlists online and order from your
favorite music retailer at
halleonard.com

CHRISTMAS COLLECTIONS
FROM HAL LEONARD
ALL BOOKS ARRANGED FOR PIANO, VOICE & GUITAR

THE BEST CHRISTMAS SONGS EVER
69 all-time favorites: Auld Lang Syne • Coventry Carol • Frosty the Snow Man • Happy Holiday • It Came Upon the Midnight Clear • O Holy Night • Rudolph the Red-Nosed Reindeer • Silver Bells • What Child Is This? • and many more.
00359130 ....$29.99

THE BIG BOOK OF CHRISTMAS SONGS
Over 120 all-time favorites and hard-to-find classics: As Each Happy Christmas • The Boar's Head Carol • Carol of the Bells • Deck the Halls • The Friendly Beasts • God Rest Ye Merry Gentlemen • Joy to the World • Masters in This Hall • O Holy Night • Story of the Shepherd • and more.
00311520 ....$22.99

CHRISTMAS SONGS – BUDGET BOOKS
100 holiday favorites: All I Want for Christmas Is You • Christmas Time Is Here • Feliz Navidad • Grandma Got Run Over by a Reindeer • I'll Be Home for Christmas • Last Christmas • O Holy Night • Please Come Home for Christmas • Rockin' Around the Christmas Tree • We Need a Little Christmas • What Child Is This? • and more.
00310887 ....$15.99

CHRISTMAS MOVIE SONGS
34 holiday hits from the big screen: All I Want for Christmas Is You • Believe • Christmas Vacation • Do You Want to Build a Snowman? • Frosty the Snow Man • Have Yourself a Merry Little Christmas • It's Beginning to Look like Christmas • Mele Kalikimaka • Rudolph the Red-Nosed Reindeer • Silver Bells • White Christmas • You're a Mean One, Mr. Grinch • and more.
00146961 ....$19.99

CHRISTMAS PIANO SONGS FOR DUMMIES®
56 favorites: Auld Lang Syne • Away in a Manger • Blue Christmas • The Christmas Song • Deck the Hall • I'll Be Home for Christmas • Jingle Bells • Joy to the World • My Favorite Things • Silent Night • more!
00311387 ....$19.95

CHRISTMAS POP STANDARDS
22 contemporary holiday hits, including: All I Want for Christmas Is You • Christmas Time Is Here • Little Saint Nick • Mary, Did You Know? • Merry Christmas, Darling • Santa Baby • Underneath the Tree • Where Are You Christmas? • and more.
00348998 ....$14.99

CHRISTMAS SING-ALONG
40 seasonal favorites: Away in a Manger • Christmas Time Is Here • Feliz Navidad • Happy Holiday • Jingle Bells • Mary, Did You Know? • O Come, All Ye Faithful • Rudolph the Red-Nosed Reindeer • Silent Night • White Christmas • and more. Includes online sing-along backing tracks.
00278176 Book/Online Audio $24.99

100 CHRISTMAS CAROLS
Includes: Away in a Manger • Bring a Torch, Jeannette, Isabella • Coventry Carol • Deck the Hall • The First Noel • Go, Tell It on the Mountain • I Heard the Bells on Christmas Day • Joy to the World • O Come, All Ye Faithful (Adeste Fideles) • Silent Night • Sing We Now of Christmas • and more.
00310897 ....$19.99

100 MOST BEAUTIFUL CHRISTMAS SONGS
Includes: Angels We Have Heard on High • Baby, It's Cold Outside • Christmas Time Is Here • Do You Hear What I Hear • Grown-Up Christmas List • Happy Xmas (War Is Over) • I'll Be Home for Christmas • The Little Drummer Boy • Mary, Did You Know? • O Holy Night • White Christmas • Winter Wonderland • and more.
00237285 ....$29.99

POPULAR CHRISTMAS SHEET MUSIC: 1980-2017
40 recent seasonal favorites: All I Want for Christmas Is You • Because It's Christmas (For All the Children) • Breath of Heaven (Mary's Song) • Christmas Lights • The Christmas Shoes • The Gift • Grown-Up Christmas List • Last Christmas • Santa Tell Me • Snowman • Where Are You Christmas? • Wrapped in Red • and more.
00278089 ....$22.99

A SENTIMENTAL CHRISTMAS BOOK
27 beloved Christmas favorites, including: The Christmas Shoes • The Christmas Song (Chestnuts Roasting on an Open Fire) • Christmas Time Is Here • Grown-Up Christmas List • Have Yourself a Merry Little Christmas • I'll Be Home for Christmas • Somewhere in My Memory • Where Are You Christmas? • and more.
00236830 ....$14.99

ULTIMATE CHRISTMAS
100 seasonal favorites: Auld Lang Syne • Bring a Torch, Jeannette, Isabella • Carol of the Bells • The Chipmunk Song • Christmas Time Is Here • The First Noel • Frosty the Snow Man • Gesù Bambino • Happy Holiday • Happy Xmas (War Is Over) • Jingle-Bell Rock • Pretty Paper • Silver Bells • Suzy Snowflake • and more.
00361399 ....$24.99

A VERY MERRY CHRISTMAS
39 familiar favorites: Blue Christmas • Feliz Navidad • Happy Xmas (War Is Over) • I'll Be Home for Christmas • Jingle-Bell Rock • Please Come Home for Christmas • Rockin' Around the Christmas Tree • Santa, Bring My Baby Back (To Me) • Sleigh Ride • White Christmas • and more.
00310536 ....$14.99

HAL•LEONARD®

Complete contents listings available online at www.halleonard.com

PRICES, CONTENTS, AND AVAILABILITY SUBJECT TO CHANGE WITHOUT NOTICE.

R